When Mourning Dawns

BOOKS BY JAMES E. MILLER

What Will Help Me? / How Can I Help?
When You're Ill or Incapacitated / When You're the Caregiver
How Will I Get Through the Holidays?
One You Love Is Dying
When You Know You're Dying
Winter Grief, Summer Grace
Autumn Wisdom
The Caregiver's Book
Welcoming Change
A Pilgrimage Through Grief
Helping the Bereaved Celebrate the Holidays
A Little Book for Preachers
Effective Support Groups
The Rewarding Practice of Journal Writing
One You Love Has Died
When a Man Faces Grief / A Man You Know Is Grieving
Finding Hope

VIDEOTAPES BY JAMES E. MILLER

Invincible Summer
Listen to Your Sadness
How Do I Go On?
Nothing Is Permanent Except Change
By the Waters of Babylon
We Will Remember
Gaining a Heart of Wisdom
Awaken to Hope
Be at Peace
The Natural Way of Prayer
You Shall Not Be Overcome
The Grit and Grace of Being a Caregiver
Why Yellow?
Common Bushes Afire

When Mourning Dawns

*Living Your Way Fully
Through the Seasons of Your Grief*

James E. Miller

To Tony,
with love.

Copyright 2000 by James E. Miller

This limited edition licensed by
special permission of Augsburg Fortress.

Willowgreen Publishing
10351 Dawson's Creek Blvd., Suite B
Fort Wayne, Indiana 46825
219/490-2222

Library of Congress Control Number:
00-133756

ISBN 1-885933-31-2

She said at length,
feeling the doctor's eyes,
"I don't know what you do exactly
when a person dies."

EDNA ST. VINCENT MILLAY
"SONNETS FROM AN UNGRAFTED TREE"

CONTENTS

Someone you know has died.
Maybe they died recently,
  or maybe it was a while ago.
Maybe it's one person you're remembering right now,
  or maybe it's several people.
Maybe it's someone you've been very close to,
  or maybe you didn't realize how close you were
    until they were gone.
Whoever it is,
  chances are life has lost some of its sparkle for you,
    some of its interest,
      maybe some of its meaning.
You may even wonder
  if life has lost *all* its meaning.
Sometimes that happens to people
  as they first begin to grieve.

When your relationship with this person first began,
you probably did not give much thought
to when your relationship would eventually end,
or where, or how.
You probably did not think about
how you would act when this happened,
or what you would feel,
or where you would turn.
You probably did not consider
what would happen to your daily routines,
or to your nightly rituals,
or to those regular anniversaries of your heart.
You did not know because you *could* not know—
you had not been through it before.
Even if you have been through *other* losses in your life,
you have never made your way through *this* loss.
And you have never made your way
as the person you are *today*,
and with all that is happening to you *now*.
You did not know what this death would *be* like,
what it would *feel* like,
and now you are learning.

You're probably aware
   that there are different theories about how grief works,
      about the things that happen to you as you grieve,
         about the order in which these things will happen.
You may find that you are being given various ideas
      about "the right way to grieve."
You may find that you're given these ideas
      whether you ask for them or not.
You may be asking yourself right now
      what the "right way" really is.
Fortunately, there is an answer for your question.
We'll deal with what the right way is
      a few pages from here.
Throughout this book
   I'll be offering you some ideas about grieving
         that have come from people
            who have taken this journey before you:
         people who, like you, have known both love and loss.
If there is one message that these people offer
      time and again, it is this:
         grief helps you.

Grief is a natural, normal, instinctive way
of coming to grips with the loss
of someone or something you love.
Grief helps you grapple with this blow you have been dealt
so that it doesn't always set you back
the way it did at first.
Your grief has one very important purpose—
to help you return to life and to go on living
so that you can find purpose again in your days,
and fulfillment,
and even joy.
Now, depending on where you are in your grief,
you may wonder if that can ever happen for you.
That's not unusual.
But know this: I believe you *can* return to life.
Grieving people have taught me that
thousands of times through the years.
I have learned it in my own life as well.
And now I want to share some of those learnings with you.
This one thought will be central to our exploration:
grieving is as natural as nature itself.

Grieving is as natural as the turning of the seasons:
the turning from summer to autumn
when autumn's time has come;
the turning from autumn to winter,
from winter to spring,
and finally from spring into summer again.
This understanding of grief will make its way
throughout the pages that follow.
We'll look at grief's four seasons in order,
each season with its own chapter.
Within each chapter,
a series of quotations, words of wisdom from the ages,
will introduce a topic of interest.
At the end of each chapter,
specific suggestions will be offered
for making your way through that particular season.
I hope this format will help you as you make your way
through the days that lie before you.
And I both hope and believe
that the dawn of your mourning
will lead eventually to a dawn in your life.

James E. Miller

AUTUMN

The long sobs
Of the violins
Of autumn
Pierce my heart.

PAUL VERLAINE

Autumn has a sob to it,
  a cry, a moan.
It is the sob of parting,
  the cry of losing,
    the moan of something ending.
What was once green with growth
  loses that color.
That which was once full of life
  begins to decline and wither.
That which once looked abundant and rich
  now begins to take on another look,
    a look that's more sparse, more spare.
When a significant death occurs in *your* life,
  something similar happens to *you*.
You lose *your* color,
  your vibrancy,
    your vitality.
You wither too.

The presence of that absence
is everywhere.

EDNA ST. VINCENT MILLAY

Early in your grief,
   and sometimes even later too,
      it's not uncommon for you to feel
   that your loss is everywhere around you,
      every place you turn,
         every direction you look.
It's also not uncommon
   for you to experience a sense of shock.
You may feel frozen and numb,
   or maybe confused and disoriented.
You may disbelieve that the one you love
   has really died.
For awhile you may talk about them
   as if they're still alive.
You may find that your feelings overwhelm you.
Then again, you may find
   that the only way for you to deal with your feelings
      is to try not to feel, temporarily at least.
Often the only way to grasp the awful truth
   of what has happened
      is ever so gradually,
         little by little,
            piece by piece,
               hurt by hurt.

And ever has it been
that love knows not its own depth
until the hour of separation.

KAHLIL GIBRAN

The death of someone dear
is an experience unlike any other.
You may feel sad,
even incredibly sad,
perhaps sadder than you thought possible.
You may feel afraid—
afraid of what's happened already,
afraid of what's happening now,
or afraid of what's to come.
You may become angry,
sometimes for no apparent reason,
and sometimes for every reason in the world.
You may want to lash out at others who don't understand,
or at those who don't help,
or at those who don't appreciate all that they have.
You may be angry at yourself
for not dealing with all this better than you are.
You may even be angry at the one who died
and left you so alone,
whether you understand that reaction or not.
You may be angry at God,
for what it appears God has done,
or *not* done.

19

Thought is deeper than all speech,
Feeling deeper than all thought.

CHRISTOPHER PEARSE CRAUCH

You may feel guilty about something you said or did,
  or something you wish you had said or done,
    or something you felt,
      or something you wish you *could* have felt.
You may feel anxious and nervous.
You're likely to feel rather empty,
    rather weak,
      rather weary.
It's possible you'll feel lonely
  in a way you've never quite known,
      even when others are around,
        sometimes *especially* when others are around.
Early in your grief
  you're likely to ride a rollercoaster of emotions.
One moment you feel as if you're doing okay—
    you feel secure and stable.
"I can handle this," you think.
Then the next moment, without warning,
    you're suddenly *in*secure and very *un*stable.
"How can I possibly get through this?" you wonder.
One moment, you feel quiet and peaceful,
    and the next moment, you're at your wit's end.
That's often how grief works.

Sorrow makes us all children again.
RALPH WALDO EMERSON

Grief can affect you in many different ways.
You may feel a tightness in your throat,
    or a heaviness across your chest,
        or a literal pain in your heart.
You may have stomachaches or headaches,
    hot flashes or cold chills,
        dizziness or shakiness.
You may have no appetite, or a huge one.
You may find it hard to sleep,
    or you may sleep much more than normal.
You may have odd dreams or frightening nightmares.
You may become unusually restless,
    moving from one activity to another,
        and often not finishing one before starting the next,
            without even knowing why.
You may look for or listen for the one who has died,
    even though deep inside you know they cannot be there.
Whatever else it is,
    grief, as it begins at least, is usually an unbalanced time.
Many people, in fact, wonder
    if they're going a little crazy as they grieve.
That's not just a common reaction—
    it's something that can be expected.
For this is a crazy period in your life, a very unusual time,
    and if you act too usual in a time that's really *unusual*,
        well, that's *unusual!*

Grief is a matter of relativity;
the sorrow should be estimated
by its proportion to the sorrower;
a gash is as painful to one
as an amputation is to another.
PERCY BYSSHE SHELLEY

We're coming now to that question
about the "right way" of grieving.
There *is* no single right way—
no one way that works for everyone.
Everyone grieves a little differently.
No one else in the world, no matter who they are,
has had your same relationship with the one who died.
No one else has your same temperament.
No one else has your exact outlook
on the world and on life.
No one else has all your previous experiences
with love and with loss.
No one else has your unique ways of dealing with stress.
And make no doubt about it: grief *is* a stress.
In fact, it can be one of the most stressful things
you'll ever do.
The bottom line is this: no one else is you!
They *cannot* be you.
So the best way for you to move through your time of loss
is in your own original way,
learning as you go,
opening to what has happened to you
as you are able.

22

IF YOU'RE IN THE AUTUMN OF YOUR GRIEF...

Following are a few suggestions for you, should you be one who finds yourself near the beginning of your time of mourning, in what we're calling the autumn of your grief.

☐ *DO WHAT COMES NATURAL.*

Be yourself—don't try to be someone else. Chances are you're not going to grieve as other people around you grieve, or as other people in your family grieve. And you will not grieve *this* time exactly as you grieved *last* time. You will have changed. You may grieve quietly, or methodically, or dramatically. You may grieve with many tears, or few tears, or no tears. You may grieve without even looking like you're grieving. Especially as you begin, don't worry about how you grieve, or how you look as you grieve, or about how you're supposed to grieve. Just do what seems right for you. Grieve as your grief comes to you.

☐ *GIVE YOURSELF PERMISSION TO FEEL WHATEVER YOU FEEL.*

In grief there are no "right feelings" or "wrong feelings." There are simply "feelings." They're not good or bad—they simply are. They're a sign that you have loved someone, and now that person has died, and now you hurt, and maybe you feel a little lost. Perhaps it's even stronger than that—maybe you feel a *lot* lost. When that happens, emotions tend to surface. So don't push your feelings aside. Give them the room they deserve. Let them have whatever space they need.

□ *FEEL FREE TO EXPRESS YOURSELF.*

If you're afraid, it's okay to say it. If you're depressed, it's okay to admit it. If you're anxious, it's okay to show it. If you're angry, it's okay to let that be known. It's better to let your feelings flow out of you, rather than to keep them stuffed inside you. That's what feelings want to do anyway—they want to get out in the open air.

□ *EXPRESS YOURSELF IN YOUR OWN WAY.*

You may be a person who's been very verbal with your feelings in the past. Then *continue* to be that way, if it feels right, especially now. Maybe you're a person who, because of the way you've been raised, or because of your natural disposition, is more reserved with how you express yourself. That's okay too. Some people can grieve without talking about it a lot. If you're good at crying, then cry. If you're a writer, try writing. If you're someone who mulls things over, then go ahead and mull—just be clear with yourself what you're mulling about. You can express your grief with music, artwork, physical activity, doing something that reminds you of the one you love, prayer, and many other ways. Find the ones that work for you. Then follow through.

□ *ALLOW YOURSELF TO LEAN.*

Early in your grief, so much is happening: so many changes, so many decisions, so much that has to be learned first-hand. That can create a lot of pressure on you. At a time when you're already tired, perhaps when you're not sleeping so well, you may not be fully yourself. You may find it hard to think clearly. You may find it difficult even to complete your day-to-day chores. If that happens, allow other people to support you. Let them do those things that can really help you. And remember that when those who love you are helping you, it's also helping *them*, because then they're able to do at least *some*thing. When your thinking feels fuzzy, turn to someone you trust and ask them if it looks fuzzy to them. When you're unsure about the next best step, turn to someone who's wise, or someone who's been there. When you feel fragile, turn to someone who's good at giving you a sense of security. Don't try to go it alone as you grieve. It makes a real difference when someone goes with you. In fact, it can make all the difference in the world.

WINTER

Two evils, monstrous either one apart,
Possessed me, and were long and loath at going:
A cry of Absence, Absence in the heart,
And in the wood the furious winter blowing.

JOHN CROWE RANSOME

Winter can seem a monstrous season of the year,
    sometimes blustery and cold,
        sometimes dreary and dark,
        often lasting longer than you want it to.
This can also be true of the winter of your grief—
    days grow tedious, nights grow longer,
        the air seems chillier than you wish.
Any shock or numbness which protected you earlier
    usually begins to wear off as your wintertime approaches.
In the starkness before you,
    you cannot avoid what lies around you:
        all you miss and all you long for,
            all your hurt and all your sadness.
Your loneliness can be piercing.
For not only are you separated from the one you love,
    but you can also feel distanced from those around you,
        and perhaps even isolated from yourself.
The emptiness of your winter can be unsettling.
The silence can be deafening.
While it may not seem so at first,
    this season of your grief is giving you something you need,
        even if you don't quite believe that yet,
            even if you don't understand how that could be.

One must not always think so much
about what one should do,
but rather what one should be.
MEISTER ECKHART

The winter of your grief
　　is a time to allow yourself simply to be.
A part of you may wish to push ahead.
Winter says, "Take your time."
A part of you may want to put your grief behind you
　　as quickly as possible.
Winter says, "Some things cannot be hurried."
A part of you may wish to avoid this season entirely.
Winter says, "Despite what you may feel,
　　this is what you need right now."
This in-between time offers a built-in opportunity
　　to do what you might not often do:
　　　　to stop and be very quiet,
　　　　　　to pause and be fully present,
　　　　　　　　to sit and be especially attentive,
　　　　　　　　　　to walk and be unusually aware.
You can let the stillness that surrounds you speak to you,
　　and it *does* have messages.
You can let the starkness that is around you teach you,
　　and it *does* have its wisdom.
In short, you can make this time of barrenness
　　an important part of your progress toward healing.
It's a time you can use to gather yourself.
But that's not all.
This is also a time you can be gathered.

You are healed of a suffering only by experiencing it to the full.
MARCEL PROUST

If you're like most people, you'll feel not much is going on
during the winter of your grief.
You may feel life is passing you by, or you're going nowhere.
But that's not the case—much *is* going on within you,
but you may not recognize that readily or easily.
Just as fields of whiteness
can hide what is happening deep underground,
so your days of quietness and sadness
can mask what is shifting deep inside you.
As you make your adjustments to this new life day by day,
you prepare yourself little by little
for how you'll go on from here.
You're likely now to visit other losses you've known,
especially other deaths you've experienced.
You're likely also to face those *additional* losses
that come as a result of this loss.
In addition to losing this one you love, for instance,
you may be losing family life as you've known it,
or you may be releasing certain roles you've enjoyed,
or certain pleasures you've become accustomed to.
You may lose friendships with those who have difficulty
making all these new transitions with you.
Your loss may affect where you live and how you live,
how you work, how you play, how you love.
However much you do not wish to make these adjustments,
still they must in time be made.
This season teaches you that these adjustments *can* be made.

31

When a person is born, we rejoice.
When they're married, we jubilate.
When they die, we try to pretend nothing happened.

MARGARET MEAD

One of the hard truths you may experience
is that our culture does not handle grief very well at all.
We're uncomfortable around it.
Any discomfort we feel is easily communicated to people
like you as you grieve.
Friends and neighbors may not talk about what has happened,
thinking that if they do, they'll upset you.
They may even avoid you, not knowing what to say or do.
Some people may try to speed you through your grief,
acting as if it shouldn't take as long as it's taking.
You'll have to decide how you'll deal with these situations.
Maybe you'll be forgiving of those who don't help you.
Maybe you'll be angry with them.
Maybe you'll be straightforward with them.
Maybe you'll just avoid them.
Or maybe you'll do all those things at one time or another
as you do your mourning.
Whatever else you do, stick up for your right to grieve.
And stick up for the fact
that your grief will take the time it needs.
Don't let people steal your grief from you.
When the time is right,
you can give it up on your own.
Until then, claim it for what it is—*yours.*

32

Call the world, if you please,
'The Vale of Soul-making.'
Then you will find out the use of the world.

JOHN KEATS

English author John Keats wrote those words
　　at the age of 23,
　　　　after watching his brother die of tuberculosis,
　　　　　　realizing that he would soon die that way himself.
The winter of your grief can be that kind of a time—
　　a vale, a valley, a low point.
A time when you ask difficult questions:
　　"Why did this have to happen?"
　　　　"Why the one I love?"
　　　　　　"Why now?"
　　　　　　　　"Why me?"
A time when you desperately want some answers,
　　and you find there may not be any,
　　　　at least not now, not yet.
A time when you feel pulled and stretched,
　　perhaps more than you thought possible.
A time when matters of the spirit come to the fore.
A time of soul-*testing*,
　　but also, as Keats says, a time of soul-*making*.
It is not an easy time—times of growth seldom are.
But it *is* a very significant time,
　　a time that can lead you
　　　　more and more toward your future.

IF YOU'RE IN THE WINTER OF YOUR GRIEF...

Here are six suggestions for going through what many people consider to be the long, cold period of their grief. These ideas can help you make the most of a time that you may not enjoy but you may still find value in.

☐ *TAKE GOOD CARE OF YOURSELF.*
Some people are so deep in their grief that they forget to take care. Others lose all desire to do it. Still others think it's selfish to care for one's own needs. But it's not. It's a critically important dimension of your return to life. When you're healthy physically, you're more apt to be healthy emotionally and mentally and spiritually. Taking care of yourself helps you stay fit for the hard labor of grief. And without question, grief *is* hard work. So take care by eating well and drinking wisely. Get your rest, and also get your exercise. Be gentle as far as what you expect of yourself. Treat yourself as you would someone you love dearly. You deserve that all of the time, but you deserve it especially as you grieve.

☐ *SETTLE INTO THE QUIET.*
Try not to run from this quiet period, but stay with it for awhile. Give it some time and it can become a soothing period. It can be a space in which you reflect upon all that has happened, both what has hurt you and what is helping you, where you've been but also where you might be going. It can be a time in which you ponder the meaning of it all. It can be a little getaway from the pressures you feel around

you. And it can be a chance to experience the truth that some things are too deep for words. In the quietness you can leave words behind as you draw closer to that which is real and true.

☐ *IF YOU HAVEN'T YET, FIND SOMEONE TO BE WITH NOW AND AGAIN.*

And if you *have* found someone already, keep being with them. You don't have to bare your soul each time you're together. You don't even have to mention your grief unless you want to. But research demonstrates that when you have someone with whom you can just be yourself as you grieve, chances are good you'll heal more naturally, with fewer complications and with more confidence. And the other person, in addition to supporting you and witnessing what is happening to you, can also offer you their perspective about the changes they see in you, and the growth. That's a perspective you cannot have when you're so immersed in all that has happened and all that continues to happen.

☐ *TURN TO SOURCES OF WISDOM.*

You might not have been ready for this before now. Your mind might be too cloudy. Your energy might be too scattered. But all along and all around is wisdom that can help you. There are people who have taken the journey through grief before you and many are willing to share what they know, if you think that would help you. There are support groups for people with losses like yours. There are books and articles and videotapes full of both information and inspiration. Grief counselors offer their specialized

36

knowledge. Funeral homes often provide helpful services and programs. Chaplains and clergy can open a spiritual dimension to this experience. So can members of your faith community, if you're a part of one. So can people with whom you feel spiritually attuned, whatever their faith. You can find a wisdom deep within as you journal, or as you pay attention to your dreams, or as you meditate. You can find a wisdom far beyond as you read, as you listen, as you pray. Whatever sources of wisdom you seek, do not forget this: grief is not an illness. It is not at all a sign that something is *wrong* with you. Grief is a sign that something is *right* with you—you've lost someone dear and now you're finding ways to regroup and go on. Your grief is teaching you that you can and you will. There is a lot of wisdom out there to show you how.

☐ *BE IN NATURE.*
Make time to walk outside or be outside several times a week, if not every day. And if that's not possible, then find ways to bring nature in to you—with flowers, plants, leaves, pictures, sounds. There is a wonderful beauty to nature that can inspire you. There is an ongoing energy to nature that can inform you. There is a grand design behind nature that can give you hope.

☐ *INCLUDE THE ONE YOU LOVE.*
This is not a time to forget the one who has died, nor is it a time to push them out of your life. It's a time to *remember* them. It's a time to recall what they have meant to you, and how much they mean to you still. It's a time to speak their

name, to display their picture, and to touch their keep-sakes, if that feels comforting to you. It is not at all morbid to do *any* of those things. There is a sense in which the one you love can be with you as you grieve, if you let them, if you want them. That can include writing to them, talking with them in your own way, feeling them around you sometimes as you go about your days. In many different ways, you don't have to go through this time alone.

SPRING

And time remembered is grief forgotten
And frosts are slain and flowers begotten,
And in the green underwood and cover
Blossom by blossom the spring begins.
ALGERNON CHARLES SWINBURNE

There is a fragility to spring's beginnings.
Tiny shoots of green emerge, as if tentatively,
   and they seem only paper thin, which they are!
Wonderful splashes of pastel appear,
   hinting that more color is on its way.
Buds open slowly, gently, gradually.
Sometimes spring comes with such subtlety
   you can almost miss it.
But as you watch for it and make yourself available to it,
   spring eventually comes with no mistaking it.
The sprouting and the blossoming
   bring a promise you've been waiting for—
      the promise of renewed life.
What happens around you in the springtime of the year
   is what can happen within you
      as you enter the springtime of your grief.
There comes a sense of growing radiance.
But this radiance is not just around you.
It's emanating from within you.

Die when I may, I want it said of me
by those who knew me best
that I always plucked a thistle and planted a flower,
where I thought a flower would grow.

ABRAHAM LINCOLN

The springtime of your grief will not be all brightness.
While the worst may be behind,
that does not mean that only the best will lie ahead.
There can still be thistles, even among the flowers.
You can still wish desperately
that the one you love were still beside you,
even when you're having one of your *better* days,
even when you *know* you're returning to life.
During this time you begin to have a little more freedom
with how you spend your days,
with what you do with your nights.
You can decide about those things
you want to start doing again.
You can experiment with trying those things
you've always wanted to do,
and maybe those things
you've never wanted to do until now.
You can turn your attention toward others, if you want,
realizing that you have something to give
as well as receive.
For come springtime, you *do* have things to offer
that no one else can.
No one.

Often the test of courage is not to die but to live.
VITTORIO ALFIERI

There is a line in the 118th Psalm that reads,
"I shall not die, but I shall live."
That's the theme behind the springtime of your grief:
yes, you can begin to see your way more clearly now;
yes, you *will* live.
But it's more than a discovery you make—
it's also a *decision* you make.
It's as if you're declaring,
"I shall not close down to life, whatever has happened.
I shall choose to live anew,
as the one I love would want."
You may trace that shift within you
to a particular moment in time.
You may feel a sense of optimism
that awakens with you one morning.
You may come upon a joy
that greets you in your dreams again.
You may hear a hearty laugh that surprises you,
especially when you realize it's *yours*!
Something begins to blossom.
Something uncurls and opens up—and it's *you*!
You sense your energy re-gathering around you.
You sense a focus re-forming within you.
As you lift your head,
you can see that the future is beckoning you again.
And it feels good.

Heartbreaks have a redemptive quality
that often goes unnoticed.
ROBERT VENINGA

Something more is at work as you grieve.
New life is not just a choice you make—
   it is an opportunity you are given.
This renewed sense of life
   is not something you can force exactly.
It's something you open yourself to,
   something you come to trust.
And as you learn to do that trusting,
   you take another step toward your healing.
As you learn to do that trusting,
   you can hear that word,
      and you can speak that word,
         which will make all the difference in the world.
The word is "yes,"
   and it appears in statements like these:
"Yes, I have come a long way."
"Yes, I *do* have much to live for."
"Yes, I *am* growing stronger,
   despite what I have been through,
      and *because* of what I have been through."
"Yes, even though death has taken its toll,
   I believe life can *still* be good,
      still be rich,
         still be full."
"Yes, I want to go on."

I had thought that your death
Was a waste and a destruction,
A pain of grief hardly to be endured.
I am beginning to learn
That your life was a gift and a growing
And a loving left with me.

MARJORIE HOLBURN

This is the legacy of grief's springtime.
As your outlook toward the future begins to change,
   so does your outlook toward the past.
You focus less on death and more on life—
   life the other gave you, and gives you still,
      life that grows within you, and will not be stopped.
You focus less on darkness and more on light—
   the light that glows from the other person's life,
      and the light that pulses from your own life,
         as well as the Light that shines from far beyond.
You focus less on what *did* happen
   and more on what *can* happen.
In other words, you focus less on what was taken
   and more on what you've been given.
You begin to concentrate on that gift
   that can *never* be taken.

If You're in the Spring of Your Grief...

Following are some suggestions for going through this springtime we've been referring to.

☐ *Expect and Allow Respites from Your Grief.*
This is true for the winter of your grief as well as its spring. As you progress through the seasons of your loss, there will be times when, for awhile, you forget about your grief. You may even forget for a moment about the one who died. Maybe this looking away from your loss just happens, or maybe you decide to help it happen, choosing, for instance, to do something for awhile that will distract you or engage you. Either way, it's a good thing to do. Either way, it's healthy for you to have longer and longer time periods in which your loss is not all-consuming. This does not at all mean that you love this person any less, or that you're leaving them behind in any way. It does not mean that you are running away from your feelings of loss. It simply means that you deserve to have some time *away* from your grief. Children do that quite naturally. We can all do well to learn from them.

☐ *Expect and Allow Passing Attacks of Grief.*
Even as you begin to feel better, you may find that you experience sudden surges of sadness when you least expect them. This can happen even on your better days, as well as the ones that don't feel so good. That's quite common and nothing to worry about. This sort of thing happens with most everyone. From time to time you may be "stabbed" by

your grief, out of the blue. Let these pangs come, and then let them go, and that's what they'll do—they'll go.

☐ *EXPERIMENT.*

You can't know what will work best for you as you move into the future unless you do some dabbling and then notice the results. For instance, what are the best ways to get through the holidays as you grieve? Learn what you can beforehand, and then try out various ideas as these days arrive. Stay with the ones that work, and feel free to change your plans if they don't work. What's the best way to handle the physical reminders of the one you love? Consider your options, try the ones that hold promise, and see what you learn. Ask others for their ideas if you want. Keep an open mind and an open attitude, and understand that any failures are simply another step toward narrowing in on what will eventually work for you.

☐ *REACH OUT.*

There will come a time in your grief when it seems right to begin facing out toward others more than facing in toward yourself. When it does, begin to reach out in those ways that make you uniquely you, knowing that some people reach out further than others. Maybe it will be in what you say, or what you do, or the way in which you make life a little better or a little easier for someone, taking some of the focus off yourself. You can still miss the one you love and not have that stop you from helping others. In fact, your experience of loss may help you be more sensitive and more caring in what you choose to do.

☐ *Underline Your Learnings.*

As the lessons begin to come to you out of your loss (and they *will* come), pay attention to them. Don't let them slip by unnoticed. Highlight them. Preserve them for future use. Make these lessons one of the unexpected benefits of this time—something is happening that can be a positive carry-over for the future. It all depends on what you do with what has happened to you. The choice is yours.

SUMMER

In the midst of winter I found at last
there was within myself
an invincible summer.

ALBERT CAMUS

Spring leads naturally and surely toward summer.
New shades of green begin to appear,
  plants arch their way upward and outward,
    new forms of growth emerge and take hold.
There is a sense of fullness approaching,
  a sense of completion on its way.
What happens around you in nature
  can also happen within you
    as you make your way fully through your grief.
Something takes root deep within you,
  and it holds.
Something courses through you and enlivens you,
  and it spreads.
This is not just something moving within you.
It is more than that.
It is not just *of* you.
It *is* you.

Sadness flies on the wings of the morning
and out of the heart of darkness comes the light.

JEAN GIRAUDOUX

This last season of your grief
 does not just arrive on its own—
  you encourage it to come.
It comes as a result
 of your having faced your fears and your doubts,
  your having spent time with the silence and aloneness,
   your having gone where you didn't want to go.
Once you've done that,
 you can begin to see for yourself the truth about grief:
  it is filled with paradox.
However hard it will have been for you
 to let go of what you once had,
  you come to realize
   that you don't have to let go of *everything*—
  some things you hold on to very tightly.
And sometimes even as you let go,
 after you let go,
  something comes back to you,
   never to leave again.

What we have once enjoyed and deeply loved
we can never lose,
for all that we love deeply
becomes a part of us.

HELEN KELLER

You begin to grasp new wisdom,
a wisdom that arrives only on the far side of your pain—
the hard-won wisdom about what life is truly all about,
and what life truly offers,
and how it offers it,
and the ways in which you are free to respond.
You can grasp a new and fuller appreciation
for what it is you've been given,
and for what it is you may yet give.
You can grasp a new and richer understanding of others,
as well as clearer and deeper knowledge about yourself.
However painful it is
for you to accept death's unchanging realities,
once you have done so, something changes.
For you will know something about the preciousness of life
in a way that you have not before.
And you will come to know,
hard as it may be to believe,
that within every ending there lies a beginning.
Every single time.

Now that you live here in my chest,
anywhere we sit is a mountaintop.

RUMI

Coming to the end of your grief
   is not simply a matter of saying goodbye
      to the one you love and then moving on.
There is a sense in which you *never* say goodbye,
   or a sense in which you *continue* to say hello.
For once you release this one you love from earthly time,
   you can embrace them beyond *all* time,
      and they can embrace you.
Even though they no longer walk the earth beside you
   the way they once did,
      they can walk even closer—
         they can walk *inside* you.
And you will not forget them
   because you *cannot* forget them.
They will be as near to you as your own breathing,
   as clear to you as your own seeing,
      as dear to you as your own being.
They can finally come to exist in you as pure love.
And by the time that happens
   you will be able to understand and take within yourself
      the words of an anonymous Chilean poet:

"I have loved.
I have been loved.
The sun has caressed my face.
Life, you owe nothing.
Life, we are at peace."

END NOTES

5
Edna St. Vincent Millay, *Collected Poems*, Harper, 1975.

18
Edna St. Vincent Millay, *Collected Poems*, Harper, 1975.

19
Kahlil Gibran, *The Prophet*, Wordsworth Classics, 1996.

29
John Crowe Ransome, *Chills and Fever*, Alfred A. Knopf, 1952.

44
Robert Veninga, *A Gift of Hope*, Ballantine Books, 1996.

53
Albert Camus, *L' Ele*, George Braziller, Inc.

54
Jean Giraudoux, *The Madwoman of Chaillot*, 1945.

55
Helen Keller, *The Story of My Life*, Watermill Press, 1993.

James E. Miller is a counselor, writer, photographer, and spiritual director who lives and works in Fort Wayne, Indiana. He lectures, leads workshops, and conducts retreats throughout North America, often utilizing his personal photography to illustrate his ideas. He has created many resources, including books, videotapes, and audiotapes, focusing on illness and dying, caregiving, loss and grief, older age, managing transition, spirituality, and hope. He is married to Bernie and together they have three children.

For information about his various resources, many of which can be purchased in quantity at sizable discounts, as well as about scheduling him for a speaking engagement, contact

Willowgreen
10351 Dawson's Creek Boulevard, Suite B
Fort Wayne, Indiana 46825
219/490-2222
jmiller@willowgreen.com

ORDER FORM

CALL 219-490-2222 8:00 am to 4:30 pm EST, Monday through Friday.

MAIL orders to:
Willowgreen, 10351 Dawson's Creek Blvd., Suite B, Fort Wayne, IN 46825

SEND emails to *orders@willowgreen.com*

CREDIT CARD ORDERS:
Supply VISA® or MasterCard® number, expiration date, and signature.

SHIP TO:

Name _____

Organization _____

Street Address _____

City _____

State/Province _____ Zip/Postal Code: _____

Telephone _____

☐ Check or money order enclosed.　　☐ Credit card info enclosed
☐ Please send me a catalog of all Willowgreen books, videotapes, and audiotapes

Qty.	Book Title	Price Each	Total Price
	When Mourning Dawns		

	Indiana residents sales tax	
SHIPPING/HANDLING Please double shipping charges for all foreign orders	Shipping and handling	
	Grand Total	

Total Purchase　　　　　　Add
Under $50 .... $5
$50.01 to $150 .... $6
$150.01 to $300 .... $8
$300.01 to $450 .... $10
$450.01 to $600 .... $14
Over $600 .... Please call

QUANTITY DISCOUNTS:

1 or 2 - $6.95 ea	*26 to 100 - $4.00 ea*
3 to 5 - $6.00 ea	*101 to 200 - $3.75 ea*
6 to 10 - $5.00 ea	*201 to 500 - $3.50 ea*
11 to 25 - $4.50 ea	*501 or more - $3.25 ea*